AN AUSTRALIAN OUTBACK Food Chain

A WHO-EATS-WHAT Adventure

Rebecca Hogue Wojahn Donald Wojahn

Lerner Publications Company
Minneapolis

For Eli and Cal. We hope this answers some of your questions.

There are many links in the chain that created this series. Thanks to Ann Kerns, Carol Hinz, Kitty Creswell, Danielle Carnito, Sarah Olmanson, Paul Rodeen, the staff of the L. E. Phillips Memorial Public Library and, finally, Katherine Hogue

Lerner Publications Company
A division of Lerner Publishing Group, Inc.
241 First Avenue North
Minneapolis, MN 55401 U.S.A.

Website address: www.lernerbooks.com

Library of Congress Cataloging-in-Publication Data

Wojahn, Rebecca Hogue.
    an Australian outback food chain : a who-eats-what adventure /
  by Rebecca Hogue Wojahn and Donald Wojahn.
      p.   cm. — (Follow that food chain)
    Includes bibliographical references and index.
    ISBN 978-0-8225-7499-6 (lib. bdg. : alk. paper)
    1. Food chains (Ecology)—Australia—Juvenile literature. I. Wojahn, Donald. II. Title.
QH197.W64 2009
577.540994—dc22   2008021117

Manufactured in the United States of America
1 2 3 4 5 6 – BP – 14 13 12 11 10 09

Contents

Introduction
WELCOME TO THE OUTBACK

Your small plane flies over the Outback just as morning breaks. Out the window, you see huge expanses of red earth. Nothing else as far as you can see! The Outback is the inner region of the country of Australia. It is one of the flattest and driest places on Earth.

Your plane dips down for a landing. You begin to see clumpy grass, pokey bushes, and scraggly trees. Termite mounds taller than your head poke out of the red dirt. It's a strange landscape.

But you won't just be exploring the red desert at the center of the Outback. The Outback is a big place with many different parts. On this Outback adventure, you'll see sand dunes, muddy creek beds, sheer rocky cliffs, towers of stones, and spreading trees too.

In much of the Outback, the air shimmers with intense heat during the day. Then, twelve hours later, animals shiver with cold at night. Everyone thirsts for water. The land can go months, even years, without rain. The heat and the dryness often cause huge fires across the Outback.

Australia is an island continent. It is separate from the rest of the world. Many of its creatures are unlike anything you'll see anywhere else. Here in the Outback, you'll find some of the most strange and unique animals on the planet. Frogs in cocoons, plagues of rabbits, not-so-cuddly koalas, spiky duck-billed echidnas, and bounding kangaroos all live in the Outback's different **habitats**. Come and meet just a few of them in this book.

Indian
Ocean

Arafura Sea

Coral Sea

South Pacific
Ocean

N

The Outback
AUSTRALIA

Tasmania

5

Choose a
TERTIARY CONSUMER

All the living things in the Outback are necessary for its health and survival. From the kangaroo bounding across the red earth to the crickets chirping under the eucalyptus leaves, all living things are connected. Animals and other organisms feed on and transfer energy to one another. This is called a **food chain** or a **food web**.

In food chains, the strongest **predators** are called **tertiary consumers**. They hunt other animals for food and have few natural enemies. Some of the animals they eat are called **secondary consumers**. Secondary consumers are also predators. They hunt plant-eating animals. Plant eaters are **primary consumers**.

Plants are **producers**. Using energy from the sun, they produce their own food. Plants take in nutrients from the soil. They also provide nutrients to the animals that eat them.

Decomposers are insects or **bacteria** that break down dead plants and animals. Decomposers change them into the nutrients found in the soil.

The plants and animals in a food chain depend on one another. Sometimes there's a break in the chain, such as one type of animal dying out. This loss ripples through the rest of the habitat.

Begin your journey through the Australian Outback food web by choosing a **carnivore**, or meat eater. These tertiary consumers are at the top of the food chain. That means that, for the most part, they don't have any enemies in the Outback (except for humans).

When it's time for the tertiary consumer to eat, pick its meal and flip to that page. As you go through the book, don't be surprised if you backtrack and end up where you never expected to be. That's how food webs work—they're complicated. And watch out for those dead ends! When you hit one of those, you have to go back to page 7 and start over with another tertiary consumer.

The main role an animal plays in the Australian Outback food web is identified by a color-coded shape. Here is the key to that code:

TERTIARY CONSUMER

PRODUCER

SECONDARY CONSUMER

PRIMARY CONSUMER

DECOMPOSER

To choose . . .

. . . a dingo, TURN TO PAGE 8.
. . . a saltwater crocodile, TURN TO PAGE 20.
. . . a wedge-tailed eagle, TURN TO PAGE 36.
. . . a Gould's monitor, TURN TO PAGE 49.

To learn more about an Australian Outback food web, GO TO PAGE 34.

DINGO *(Canis dingo)*

With a yip and a growl, the mother dingo sends her five pups scurrying back to the den. She's dug a hole under a log to keep the pups safe. But they're getting bigger now. They've grown bolder about straying from home.

This mother dingo and her family may look like a friendly dog with cuddly puppies. An adult dingo is about the size of a Labrador retriever, and they belong to the same family as dogs. But don't be fooled into thinking they're pets. These are definitely wild animals. You'll sometimes hear them howl at night, as wolves do. Wolves are dingoes' close relatives.

The mother dingo coughs up a fluid. She's not sick. It's water, and her puppies eagerly lick it up. It'll be the only liquid they drink on this hot day in the Outback.

Toward evening, the mother dingo gives her pups a nuzzle as they settle down. Then she leaves the den to look for supper. Outside, she's joined in the gathering darkness by two other dingoes.

Most dingoes are tan with white patches on their feet and tails. But these two are red and black. More and more often, dingoes are interbreeding, or mixing, with domestic dogs (tame dogs, such as house pets). This interbreeding means that purebred dingoes are becoming scarcer. Wildlife experts think wild purebred dingoes are in danger of becoming **extinct**.

The mother dingo sniffs at a dead animal carcass left along the road. Dingoes will eat **carrion** if they have to. She's just about to dig in when a jeep roars over a nearby hill. Its bright lights blind her. She panics.

The dingoes scatter. It turns out that they're lucky they were scared away from their meal. That carcass wasn't road kill. It was dingo bait—poisoned meat people leave out for dingoes to eat. Lots of sheep farmers hate dingoes. Dingoes will hunt and kill slow-moving sheep. So farmers often shoot or poison dingoes.

The small pack keeps moving. They'll roam just a small area tonight, but every few days, they'll shift to a new territory. They'll rotate through 32 square miles (83 square kilometers) before starting over again.

The Dingo Fence

Dingo bait isn't the only way that Australians have tried to keep dingoes off their sheep farms. In the 1880's, Australians built the world's longest fence to keep dingoes out of the southeastern part of the continent. That area is home to many of Australia's large sheep farms. The wire fence is more than 3,000 miles (5,000 km) long. It was only partly successful. Fewer dingoes are found south of the fence. But without dingoes around as predators, kangaroos and rabbits thrive. They eat a lot of the grass the sheep need to survive.

Soon they spot a young red kangaroo. It leaps mightily. But, working together, the dingoes surround it and bring it down. They take turns pulling off chunks of meat. The mother dingo gulps it down quickly.

Now, with a full tummy, she's ready to head back to the den. When she gets there, she'll throw up the meat for her pups—just as she did with the water. In the meantime, her stomach starts to digest the food. That makes it easier for her pups to eat later.

Last night for dinner, she was lucky in her hunt too. She gulped . . .

Dingoes chase a kangaroo.

. . . **a western barred bandicoot hidden in the brush.** To see what another western barred bandicoot is up to, TURN TO PAGE 50.

. . . **another red kangaroo.** To see what another red kangaroo is up to, TURN TO PAGE 40.

. . . **a northern quoll.** To see what another northern quoll is up to, TURN TO PAGE 44.

. . . **a greater bilby that poked his head out of his burrow at the wrong time.** To see what another greater bilby is up to, TURN TO PAGE 48.

. . . **emu eggs stolen from their nest.** To see what another emu is up to, TURN TO PAGE 16.

. . . **a Queensland koala, moving to a new tree.** To see what another Queensland koala is up to, TURN TO PAGE 27.

. . . **a nest of European wild rabbit babies.** To see what another European wild rabbit is up to, TURN TO PAGE 46.

. . . **a dead short-beaked echidna, hit by a car.** To see what another short-beaked echidna is up to, TURN TO PAGE 58.

FRILLED LIZARD *(Chlamydosaurus kingii)*

The young frilled lizard basks in the sun on the rocky outcrop. He's not full-grown yet, but he's been on his own since the day he hatched from his egg. And as a **reptile**, he's **cold-blooded**. The more rays he soaks up, the warmer his blood is inside him—and the faster he can move.

Other reptiles also look for the sun's warmth. A huge carpet python slithers across the rock. She came to bask. But this frilled lizard is just the right size for a meal—and she hasn't eaten in weeks. She slips closer.

Without warning, the frilled lizard opens his mouth. A collar of skin pops up like an umbrella around his face. The skin is called a frill, or a ruff. The frill makes the lizard look larger and fiercer. He hisses and rushes the python. She scoots back in alarm. But she doesn't retreat far enough. So the lizard thrashes his tail and bares his sharp teeth. He looks just like a tiny ferocious dinosaur. It's enough to scare off most animals.

This snake, however, is too hungry to be easily discouraged. She slides forward again.

The lizard spins around, raises up on his two hind legs, and races for the nearest tree. He scampers up and crouches flat on a branch. He'll have to wait out the python. But at least there's plenty to eat up here.

Last night for dinner, the lizard ate . . .

. . . crickets just hatching from their eggs. To see what other crickets are up to, TURN TO PAGE 57.

. . . bush flies hovering over a dead kangaroo. To see what other bush flies are up to, TURN TO PAGE 45.

. . . a just-hatched budgerigar. To see what another budgerigar is up to, TURN TO PAGE 32.

TAWNY FROGMOUTH
(Podargus strigoides)

That's not a broken tree limb up at the top of the tree. It's a tawny frogmouth. This large bird is snoozing, standing upright. His yellow gold eyes are closed. With his silvery gray feathers, he looks just like part of the tree. Most creatures passing by never even know he's there.

A tawny frogmouth closes its eyes and stretches out to blend in among the tree branches.

The frogmouth only stirs when his mate arrives. She'll sit on their nest of twigs while he hunts tonight. He lets out a booming cry, "Oom-oom-oom." Then he flutters to a different branch. And waits. His hunting doesn't really look all that different from his sleeping.

Frogmouths look like owls, but they aren't related. Frogmouths have short legs with weak feet. No owl-like talons for them. Frogmouths use their wide mouths and sharp beaks to catch their prey.

Below, a kangaroo mouse wanders by. It's just what the frogmouth was waiting for. He flaps down and pounces. Snap! The mouse is pinned in the frogmouth's beak. And with a quick shake and a toss against the tree, the mouse is killed. Dinnertime.

Last night for dinner, the frogmouth ate . . .

The frogmouth's wide mouth earned the bird its name. Its mouth reminded people of a frog's mouth.

. . . **a western barred bandicoot scooting from one bush to another.** To see what another western barred bandicoot is up to, TURN TO PAGE 60.

. . . **a baby ghost bat chasing a centipede.** To see what another ghost bat is up to, TURN TO PAGE 54.

. . . **a young carpet python just hatched from her egg.** To see what another carpet python is up to, TURN TO PAGE 18.

. . . **a frilled lizard looking for a place to stay warm at the end of the day.** To see what another frilled lizard is up to, TURN TO PAGE 12.

. . . **a small spectacled hare-wallaby scratching out a place to take a nap.** To see what another spectacled hare-wallaby is up to, TURN TO PAGE 30.

. . . **crickets munching on dead leaves.** To see what other crickets are up to, TURN TO PAGE 57.

. . . **a marsupial mole chomping on some grubs.** To see what another marsupial mole is up to, TURN TO PAGE 35.

EMU *(Dromaius novaehollandiae)*

The emu settles on his nest. For fifty-five days, he won't budge. No eating. No drinking. No bathroom breaks. Just sitting. But he will be rewarded. The eggs under him will change from a dark bluish green to a light grey. And then they'll be ready to hatch.

The emu shades them from the hot Outback sun with his wings. Emus don't fly, so their wings have become small and weak. But the droopy feathers that hang from the emu father's wings provide good shade.

Suddenly, a Gould's monitor appears through the brush. He's looking for an easy treat—an egg, maybe. The emu father quickly reacts. He stretches his neck out and trumpets out a booming call. His long neck makes the sound louder. Other animals can hear it almost 2 miles (3 kilometers) away.

The emu's blast scares the monitor off. He's lucky the emu father didn't get up. The emu has a mean kick and could easily kill the monitor. He goes back to tending his nest. In the commotion, an egg has rolled out. He nudges it back to the center of the nest. Just fifty-four more days to go.

When the emu is ready to eat again, he'll dine on . . .

Adult emus can grow to be 5 to 6 feet (1.5 to 1.8 meters) tall. They weigh from 65 to 120 pounds (30 to 54 kilograms).

17

. . . the scrubby brush and grass of the Outback. To see what the plants of the Outback are like, TURN TO PAGE 24.

CARPET PYTHON *(Morelia spilota)*

Thirty-five.
Thirty-six.
Thirty-seven.
Thirty-seven carpet python eggs lie inside a hollow log. They are about the size of golf balls.

The mother python snuggles her 6-foot (2-meter) body around the eggs. Her black and brown coloring looks just like the dead leaves around her. Her coiled body will keep the eggs warm and their temperature even until the snakes are born.

Like all snakes, the python is **cold-blooded**. Warm-blooded animals make their own body heat and keep their insides at a steady temperature. Cold-blooded animals draw their body heat from outside sources such as the sun. But nights are cold in the Outback. So as the sun sets, the python begins twitching her muscles. Those little movements will help raise her body temperature.

Keeping her body temperature steady helps the python to survive. It also determines whether her eggs will hatch male or female babies. The warmer she keeps the eggs, the more boy pythons she'll have.

As she rests, a dingo sniffs around outside the log. He is looking for a snack. He paws at the log and then noses the leaves in the hole. Like a whip, the python lashes out and sinks her teeth into the dingo's nose. With a yelp, the dingo retreats. The python settles back around her eggs.

Pythons are not poisonous snakes. A python hunts by sneaking up on prey and wrapping her body around it. The python squeezes the prey tight enough to kill it. Then she swallows the meal whole and lets it digest slowly.

While a python is guarding a nestful of eggs, she doesn't eat much. She uses her energy to keep the eggs warm. *But last night for dinner, this carpet python hunted and swallowed . . .*

... a spectacled hare-wallaby caught in a midmorning snooze. To see what another spectacled hare-wallaby is up to, TURN TO PAGE 30.

... a young Gould's monitor resting on a termite mound. To see what another Gould's monitor is up to, TURN TO PAGE 49.

... a marsupial mole that poked his head out at the wrong time. To see what another marsupial mole is up to, TURN TO PAGE 35.

... a budgerigar at the edge of her flock. To see what another budgerigar is up to, TURN TO PAGE 32.

... a western barred bandicoot startled out of the brush. To see what another western barred bandicoot is up to, TURN TO PAGE 56.

... an emu chick that strayed too far from the nest. To see what another emu is up to, TURN TO PAGE 16.

... a frilled lizard sunning on a rock. To see what another frilled lizard is up to, TURN TO PAGE 12.

... a tawny frogmouth pouncing on a mouse. To see what another tawny frogmouth is up to, TURN TO PAGE 14.

SALTWATER CROCODILE *(Crocodylus porosus)*

In the blistering heat of the day, the saltwater crocodile has found a cool spot. He lies submerged in the muddy water of a **billabong**. But this water hole is slowly disappearing. It's evaporating, or drying up, in the heat. In the next few weeks, the croc will have to go in search of more water.

20

In the meantime, he stretches out his 20-foot (6-meter) length and waits for another animal to come by for a drink. He'll kill most prey with a single snap of his jaws. The rest he'll drag into the water and drown.

The crocodile sees a movement on the side of the billabong. He pushes off with his feet on the muddy bottom to investigate. It's not food, it's another croc. This is a small one, searching out a new water hole after his dried up. With a flick of his tail, the big croc shoots across the small pond. With a roar, he explodes out of the water at the junior crocodile. This is *his* billabong. The smaller croc thinks about staying and fighting for only a moment. Then he retreats. The larger one chases after him for a few yards, just to be sure.

21

Saltwater crocodiles are among the world's smartest reptiles. They talk to one another using four different calls. Baby crocs chirp inside their eggs to tell the mother croc it's time to unbury them. Young hatchlings emit a distress call when they are in danger. Older adult crocs growl long and low when they're looking for a mate. They hiss and cough to announce that they want to be left alone.

Saltwater crocs, or salties as they're called in Australia, are the world's biggest and most dangerous crocodiles. They can kill large prey, including humans. In fact, people were once so scared of salties that they shot them on sight. It wasn't until the crocs were in danger of becoming **extinct** that people stopped killing them. Luckily, salties have made a strong comeback and are doing well in the wild.

Last night for dinner, this croc snapped up...

A saltwater crocodile snaps up a fish.

. . . a dingo sniffing near the water's edge. To see what another dingo is up to, TURN TO PAGE 8.

. . . a water-holding frog just burrowing up from the mud. To see what another water-holding frog is up to, TURN TO PAGE 52.

. . . a short-beaked echidna rolled into a ball. To see what another short-beaked echidna is up to, TURN TO PAGE 58.

. . . a northern quoll scampering across the sand. To see what another northern quoll is up to, TURN TO PAGE 44.

. . . a Gould's monitor skulking around for some eggs. To see what another Gould's monitor is up to, TURN TO PAGE 48.

. . . a greater bilby scratching for seeds. To see what another greater bilby is up to, TURN TO PAGE 48.

. . . a red kangaroo stopping by for a sip of water. To see what another red kangaroo is up to, TURN TO PAGE 40.

. . . a spectacled hare-wallaby emerging from his bush. To see what another spectacled hare-wallaby is up to, TURN TO PAGE 30.

PLANTS OF THE OUTBACK

Spiky, spiny, thorny. The plants of the Outback have to be able to withstand blistering sunlight, cold nights, and months—sometimes even years—without rain. They've got to be tough to survive. That means saving every last drop of water and fighting off any animals who want to snack on them.

Because of their size, trees need more water than other plants. So there just aren't many trees in the Outback. The ones that are there have survived by adapting—changing to make the most of their environment.

a baobab tree

Low wattles, or acacia trees, are sprinkled throughout the Outback. Their thorns keep away many animals that want to eat their blooms and leaves. Baobab trees have very thick trunks. They store water deep in the trunks. Sometimes Aborigines, Australia's native people, tap baobabs for a drink when they need water. Eucalyptus trees need more water to grow than other Outback trees do. But some eucalyptus types grow in dry areas. Their leaves are small and waxy to conserve, or save, water. And their smelly leaves are poisonous—to everyone but koalas.

eucalyptus leaves

carbon dioxide   oxygen

Plants make food and oxygen through photosynthesis. Plants draw in carbon dioxide (a gas found in air) and water. Then they use the energy from sunlight to turn the carbon dioxide and water into their food.

Grass is thick and tall in some parts of the Outback. In other places, it is short and patchy. Either way, it provides food and moisture for all sorts of animals. And when it does finally rain, a rainbow of flowers erupts across the floor of the Outback.

Plants can't survive without sunlight, water, and food. Plant leaves draw carbon dioxide, a gas, from the air. Their roots draw water and **nutrients** from the soil. The plants use energy from the sun to turn the carbon dioxide and water into food.

Some of the plants' food also comes from the bodies of dead animals. As the animals **decompose**, bacteria breaks the carcasses down into nutrients.

Last night for dinner, the plants' nutrients in the soil came from . . .

Flowers color the landscape after a rain.

25

. . . dead plants and leaves.

. . . the carcass of a dingo. To see what another dingo is up to, TURN TO PAGE 8.

. . . the carcass of a saltwater crocodile. To see what another saltwater crocodile is up to, TURN TO PAGE 20.

. . . bush flies that spread animal dung. To see what other bush flies are up to, TURN TO PAGE 45.

. . . the carcass of a wedge-tailed eagle. To see what another wedge-tailed eagle is up to, TURN TO PAGE 38.

. . . the carcass of a red kangaroo. To see what another red kangaroo is up to, TURN TO PAGE 40.

. . . the carcass of a ghost bat. To see what another ghost bat is up to, TURN TO PAGE 54.

. . . the carcass of a Queensland koala. To see what another Queensland koala is up to, TURN TO PAGE 27.

QUEENSLAND KOALA *(Phascolarctos cinereus adustus)*

The Queensland koala clamps down on a branch of a eucalyptus tree. The branch is high above a **billabong**. With those long claws and extra thumb, the koala is secure in her perch. She can—and does—sleep without falling out of the tree. Not much will convince her to come down. Koalas are slow moving and like to sleep—sometimes up to eighteen hours a day.

When the koala gets hungry, she leans forward to sniff a leaf with her big, extra-sensitive nose. She's a picky eater and smells each and every leaf she puts in her mouth. This leaf meets her approval. She munches it down.

Koalas are **herbivores**, or plant eaters. An adult can eat 2.5 pounds (1 kilogram) of eucalyptus leaves a day. Australia has more than six hundred kinds of eucalyptus trees.

Not a Teddy Bear

This koala may look cuddly cute with her big fluffy ears, teddy bear nose, and sleepy movements. But watch out! Her personality definitely isn't cuddly. Koalas will scratch or bite if other animals—including people—get too close. First, they make a ticking sound as a warning. Then they swipe out with those long black claws.

Maybe koalas are just frustrated that people think they're some kind of bear. Bears and koalas are not related.

After eating, the koala shifts her weight. Hugging tight to her back is her baby—a miniature version of herself.

Koalas are **marsupials**—they have pouches in which their young grow. A dime-sized newborn wiggles his way to the pouch. Once inside, he guzzles her milk until he's big enough to be introduced to the world. And when he is, he'll ride with his mom for a while until he learns all he needs to know about being a koala.

Last night for dinner, the koala sniffed and swallowed...

29

A koala with her baby munches on a eucalyptus leaf.

... only the just-right eucalyptus tree leaves. To see what the plants of the Outback are like, TURN TO PAGE 24.

SPECTACLED HARE-WALLABY
(Lagorchestes conspicillatus)

The sun scorches today. But the spectacled hare-wallaby rests comfortably in his shallow burrow under a clump of tall grass. The wallaby could hardly be better suited for the Outback's extreme climate. His two-toned fur can keep him either cool or warm. Today, the light-colored fur reflects the strong sun rays, keeping him cool.

30

And if there's no rain and no water to drink? No problem. He can get all the fluid he needs from the morning dew and the leaves he eats. He has the most efficient kidneys of any **mammal**. Kidneys help get rid of a body's wastes by flushing them out as urine. The spectacled hare-wallaby's kidneys get rid of his waste using only a tiny bit of his body's water.

Threats

Like other wallabies species, spectacled hare-wallabies are getting scarcer. Animals that are new to the Outback threaten the wallabies' safety and food. Humans have brought animals such as foxes and house cats to the Outback. These animals hunt and kill wallabies. Other nonnative animals, such as cattle and rabbits, don't eat wallabies. But they eat the grass that the wallabies eat and shelter under. Humans also change the wallaby's habitat. As humans build more houses and roads, wallabies have less shrubby space to live on.

He stretches out, panting. Panting helps the wallaby keep his temperature steady. But it also provides moisture. The air animals exhale contains water, and even that bit of moisture is reused by the wallaby. It is recycled to his stomach.

The spectacled hare-wallaby doesn't waste his energy in the heat of the day. But at dusk, he'll perk up and get his food. *Last night for dinner, the spectacled hare-wallaby chewed . . .*

. . . **grass and leaves.** He needs lots of leaves to get enough **nutrients**. To see what the plants of the Outback are like, TURN TO PAGE 24.

BUDGERIGARS *(Melopsittacus undulatus)*

The budgerigar pecks at the ground. No, he's not swallowing tiny bugs or even small seeds. He's swallowing the dirt itself. The soil contains **minerals** that his body needs.

After a quick sip of water from the **billabong**, he flits to the top of a eucalyptus tree. There, hidden in its branches, is his lifelong mate. He's a more common green and yellow budgie. She's a rarer blue. Together they've gnawed branches and shaped a nest in the tree.

She's busy these days. Now that there's been a little rain, she's been laying an egg in their nest every two days. She'll lay six to eight eggs. The eggs will hatch just as they were laid—one every two days. He's got a big job ahead of him. Once the eggs hatch, he'll take over tending them.

Around them the tree trembles with other budgerigars. They chatter and preen (groom their feathers) as they watch out for one another. When the night grows dark, they quiet down and draw close together for warmth and safety.

Last night for dinner, the budgerigar swallowed . . .

Flocks of Budgies

Budgerigars live in flocks of twenty to sixty birds. A budgie's whole life revolves around the flock. Within the flock, the birds have a strong sense of order. If one budgie flies off on his own, others will fly after him and force him to return to the group. This sense of group behavior helps budgies perform amazing feats in flight. A thousand budgies can fly in one direction in search of water. Then, without any obvious signal, all one thousand will turn and fly in another direction—without bumping into one another.

... **bush flies.** To see what other bush flies are up to, TURN TO PAGE 45.

... **a cricket or two.** To see what other crickets are up to, TURN TO PAGE 57.

AN OUTBACK FOOD WEB

In the Outback, energy moves around the food chain from the sun to plants, from plants to plant eaters, and from animals to the creatures that eat them. Energy also moves from dead animals to the plants and animals that draw nutrients from them.

MARSUPIAL MOLE *(Notoryctes typhlops)*

You may think you saw the head of a southern **marsupial** mole pop up through the sandy soil. But chances are slim that it really was one. The moles are in danger of becoming **extinct**, and this is a *DEAD END*.

Marsupial moles are scarce for many reasons. Humans once trapped them for their yellowish fur. Dingoes, wild cats, and foxes hunt them for food. And the big trucks used for transportation and mining pack down the soil so the moles can't dig.

Digging is what marsupial moles are made to do. Their whole body is built to "swim" through the sand. They use their hard noses and front paws to burrow. Their backbones are rigid to make them stronger diggers. And they are blind, so the dirt doesn't bother their eyes. Once underground, the moles hunt for their favorite food—young insects.

35

WEDGE-TAILED EAGLE (Aquila audax)

Stretching out both of her huge wings, the wedge-tailed eagle soars over the Outback. She's easy to recognize. For one thing, she's the largest bird of prey in Australia. And second, her tail has a point, or a "wedge."

The eagle makes flying look easy, but she's always adjusting her wing muscles to catch the wind better. With a few flaps, she climbs higher. She can soar up here for hours without having to flap her wings once. Now she's at 6,000 feet (1,800 meters)—that's more than 1 mile (1.6 kilometers) high! She tips her wings to turn. These few miles she's circling are her home territory. She patrols it often.

She's also scanning for prey. And there! A rabbit hops lazily along in the open. It's having a midmorning snack. The eagle angles her wings down and circles lower. Then, swooping low over the ground, she snatches the rabbit up.

That rabbit was simple stuff. She could have spotted it from 2 miles (3 km) away. Picking it up was no big deal either—she can lift half her body weight. Sometimes she gangs up with other eagles. Together, they can hunt down and dine on a full-sized kangaroo!

Wedge-tailed eagles have big wingspans—the measurement from the tip of one outstretched wing to the tip of the other. An adult female's wingspan may reach 7.5 feet (2.3 m). This eagle has used her wings to zoom down and capture a rabbit.

38

The Nest

Wedge-tailed eagles usually build huge nests in the tallest trees. But some live in parts of the Outback where there are few trees. In those cases, eagles build nests from enormous piles of sticks on the sides of rocky cliffs. An eagle pair will often add a fresh layer of sticks to the nest floor. But they're not too neat about it. Down at the bottom of the cliff you may find another big pile of sticks—pieces that they dropped while working on the nest.

Clutching the rabbit in her sharp talons, the eagle carries her prey back to her nest. Here her mate rests, keeping their two eggs warm. They'll take turns hunting until the eggs hatch in about forty-five days. Then she'll stay with them for the first thirty days while he hunts. *Last night for dinner, she shared with her mate . . .*

... a northern quoll caught out in the open. To see what another northern quoll is up to, TURN TO PAGE 44.

... a dead short-beaked echidna, hit by a car. To see what another short-beaked echidna is up to, TURN TO PAGE 58.

... a European wild rabbit crossing a clearing. To see what another European wild rabbit is up to, TURN TO PAGE 46.

... a carpet python sunning on a stone. To see what another carpet python is up to, TURN TO PAGE 18.

... a budgerigar in midflight. To see what another budgerigar is up to, TURN TO PAGE 32.

... a dingo pup playing with a lizard. To see what another dingo is up to, TURN TO PAGE 8.

... a young red kangaroo that bounded too far from his mother. To see what another red kangaroo is up to, TURN TO PAGE 40.

... a marsupial mole digging for insects. To see what another marsupial mole is up to, TURN TO PAGE 35.

RED KANGAROO (Macropus rufus)

Sproing. Sproing! The red kangaroo cruises by. Her huge back legs pump together. Her tiny front legs are curled against her chest. With each bounce, she pushes her enormous feet against the hard red earth. The tendons (strong, fiberlike tissue) in her heels act like rubber bands. The tendons stretch and snap back together. That snapping is what gives the kangaroo her spring. She has enough power to sail more than 20 feet (6 meters) with each leap. When kangaroos move, they spend most of their time in midair.

And they are made to move! When kangaroos are traveling, they don't even have to breathe. The impact of each landing squeezes the air in and out of their lungs for them.

Kangaroos can travel almost 30 miles (48 kilometers) an hour. But today, this kangaroo isn't moving at top speed. One of her babies, called a joey, hops along beside her. She moves more slowly so he can keep up.

The mother kangaroo's head suddenly bobs up. The shadow of a wedge-tailed eagle has fallen across the ground. Danger! The joey tries to somersault himself into the pouch on his mother's stomach. But she keeps the muscles around the pouch relaxed, and he tumbles back out. He looks at her, confused. Surely she won't let the eagle get him?

The mother kangaroo huddles the joey next to her for protection. But the pouch is off limits. The truth is, he's just gotten too big. And she's got a new joey in her pouch.

The red kangaroo is the world's largest marsupial. Adult males, called boomers, can stand 6 feet (2 m) tall and weigh up to 198 pounds (90 kilograms).

Kangaroos are **marsupials**. These special animals grow their babies in their stomach pouches. A few days earlier, a thumbnail-sized joey was born. Pink and hairless, the newborn joey still needs a safe place to grow. The newborn climbed up the mother's fur and into her pouch. The newborn joey will stay safe there until the joey is stronger and bigger.

Female kangaroos, called fliers, are almost always pregnant. A flier takes care of her joeys until they're about one year old. So she often has more than one baby with her. She has a baby in the womb, a young joey in the pouch, and an older joey by her side.

It's time for the older joey to learn to fend for himself. As they wait out the eagle, she licks his face. This passes on her bacteria to him. Bacteria are tiny living things that animals carry

Amazing Legs

Kangaroo legs are built for speed. Scientists have put kangaroos on treadmills and found something unusual. Unlike most other animals, kangaroos aren't strained by going top speed. They tire at top speed at the same rate they tire going more slowly. In fact, kangaroos are awkward at slow speeds. One reason is that they can't move their hind legs separately. That makes walking difficult for them. While grazing, they hobble along, using their front paws and tail for balance.

But in water, it's another story. Kangaroos suddenly can move their legs independently. And—as you might imagine with their huge feet—they are excellent swimmers.

A red kangaroo goes for a swim.

in their stomachs and mouths. The bacteria will help the joey digest the grass he eats. Kangaroos are **herbivores**—they eat only plants. This kangaroo and her joey will munch on grass all day long. The grass does not have much nutrition. So they have to eat a lot of it to survive.

The joey rips the tough grass leaves up. Kangaroos' jaws come in two parts, with a stretchy band between them. With each mouthful, the sides of the joey's lower jaw come apart. This allows him to get a bigger mouthful.

Inside his mouth, he grinds the grass against ridged molars, or back teeth. When the molars wear down, they fall out and the teeth behind them move into

A young kangaroo licks its front paws.

43

place. At some point, the kangaroo runs out of new teeth. He can't eat anymore and will die. But most kangaroos don't live long enough to run out of teeth.

Next to him, his mother pants. The sun and the temperature are rising. Soon it'll be time for a snooze. They'll eat again when the sun goes down. With her back paws, she scratches out a hollow in the dirt. It'll be cooler here. The joey joins her. They start licking again. This time they concentrate on their front legs. It's not just that they want to keep clean. Their front paws have extra blood vessels. Keeping that skin moist actually cools their whole bodies. And they can use all the help they can get. It'll reach 110°F (43°C) today in the Outback.

Last night for dinner, the mother kangaroo and her joey ground up . . .

. . . more leaves and grass.
To see what the plants of the Outback are like, TURN TO PAGE 24.

NORTHERN QUOLL *(Dasyurus hallucatus)*

The northern quoll pounces on a toad. It's just the right size for dinner for this **marsupial**. Frogs and toads are the quoll's favorite meal. But this toad is bad news. This is a cane toad, and it is very poisonous. The northern quoll doesn't know it as he chews on the toad, but he's doomed. This is a *DEAD END*.

   People brought cane toads to Australia in 1935. Beetles (a type of bug) were damaging Australia's sugarcane fields. People released the toads into the fields to eat the beetles. But the toads soon overran the regions they were released in. Unlike Australia's native frogs and toads, cane toads kill most animals that eat them. They endanger not just northern quolls but many other animals too.

44

BUSH FLIES *(Musca vetustissima)*

A female bush fly buzzes straight up a resting dingo's nose. The dingo sneezes, and the fly is shot back out. She buzzes back to land on his eye. He shakes her off. She flits to a scrape on his paw. The dingo gives up and lets her land.

If there were just a few bush flies, this one wouldn't seem so annoying. But there are millions just like her. Everywhere you go in the Outback, swarms of flies follow. Bush flies are a way of life in Australia.

That female fly is pesky and determined for a reason. She needs to get protein, a chemical substance used by the body. Without protein, she can't lay her eggs. And the only way for her to get protein is from animals' tears, spit, nose, blood, sweat, urine, or poop. If she weren't so persistent, her species wouldn't survive.

After getting her protein, she's off again. She's looking for a place to lay her eggs. Lucky for her, there's dingo dung, or poop, nearby. It's the perfect home for her eggs. Within just a few hours, they'll hatch into dung-eating **maggots**. Then it'll be time for them to burrow underground. They'll continue to grow underground until they emerge as the next generation of bush flies.

Bush flies are decomposers. They eat dead plants and help break the plants down into **nutrients**. The flies leave those nutrients in the soil for other plants and animals to use.

Last night for dinner, the bush fly maggots ate . . .

45

. . . **the leftover bits of plants and grass in the dung.** To see what the plants of the Outback are like, **TURN TO PAGE 24.**

EUROPEAN WILD RABBIT *(Oryctolagus cuniculus)*

With his long incisor teeth, the European wild rabbit crunches down on a tuft of grass. When it's gone, he scratches at the dirt. Ah, more of the tasty plant. He nibbles the roots. By the time he hops away, he's eaten the whole plant. There's nothing left for new grass to grow back from.

Rabbits aren't native to Australia. In the 1700s and 1800s, European settlers brought rabbits to southeastern Australia. Rabbits breed quickly, and the population swelled. Within years, millions of rabbits swarmed across the southern and central parts of the continent.

The huge rabbit population is very destructive to the environment. The rabbits destroy grass and native plants, leaving little behind for other animals. Rabbits are to blame for several mammal species becoming **extinct**. Other species of animals and plants are **endangered** by the rabbit.

The Rabbit-Proof Fence

In 1901 Australians began building a 2,023-mile (3,256-kilometer) rabbit-proof fence across Western Australia. The fence was built to be high enough so rabbits couldn't jump over it. And it was sunk deep enough in the ground that rabbits couldn't dig under it. But like other rabbit-controlling ideas, it wasn't very successful. Rabbits slipped by to the other side before it was finished in 1907.

The rabbit's destruction of plants also causes soil erosion. With no plant roots to hold the soil in place, it blows away. This erosion has damaged Australian farming practices.

To try to control the wild rabbit population, Australians have hunted the animals and poisoned their warrens, or dens. People have also purposely introduced diseases into the rabbit population.

These methods have killed large numbers of rabbits. But a female rabbit can have five litters of four to five rabbits a year. And those rabbits can start having their own babies when they are just four months old. It's hard to control an animal population that grows that fast. Australians continue to look for solutions to their rabbit problem.

Baby rabbits play just outside their warren.

47

In the meantime, this rabbit continues to eat. *Last night for dinner, he devoured . . .*

. . . **grass, brush, and the leaves on bushes and trees.** To see what the plants of the Outback are like, TURN TO PAGE 24.

GREATER BILBY *(Macrotis lagotis)*

Sorry, this is a *DEAD END*! The greater bilby is **endangered** in parts of Australia and threatened in others. Just one hundred years ago, this cat-sized **marsupial** was found across the Outback. It slept in sandy burrows by day and foraged for seeds and insects at night. In the 2000s, there were fewer than one thousand greater bilbies left.

It's been difficult trying to save the bilbies. Cattle and other livestock push them out of their habitats. But one of the worst problems is feral cats. Feral cats are pet house cats that have turned wild. The feral cats breed and multiply. Now there are seventeen million feral cats in Australia. And they often love to hunt bilbies.

Lesser Bilby

Wildlife experts hope the greater bilby won't go the way of its close relative, the lesser bilby. The lesser bilby has been extinct since the 1950s. The last trace of the rabbit-eared mini-kangaroo lookalike was a skull found under a wedge-tailed eagle's nest in 1967. The skull was less than fifteen years old. But there's been no trace of lesser bilbies since then.

GOULD'S MONITOR *(Varanus gouldii)*

With a flick of his strong claws, the Gould's monitor slashes open a termite mound. This large lizard is looking for an easy place to rest. And someplace hidden is the safest spot for him. As he digs out a space in the termite mound, a dingo approaches. The dingo just ate and isn't looking for prey. And this monitor is almost 4 feet (1.2 meter) long—a little too big for a meal anyway. The dingo is just curious.

But the monitor doesn't know that. He sees the curious dingo as a danger. The monitor raises his long neck. He flicks his forked tongue in and out. He hisses a warning. The dingo retreats a little, but not far enough for the monitor. Balancing with his tail, the monitor rears up on his hind legs. He's mad and scared. He charges the dingo.

Goannas

Monitor lizards thrive in the Outback. Everywhere you look is a different kind sunning on a rock. Australians also call the lizards goannas. It's thought that the word *goanna* comes from *iguana*. The first European settlers saw the monitors and thought they looked like iguanas—another kind of lizard.

The dingo jogs away, looking over his shoulder. Whew! The monitor relaxes and drops back down on all fours. But then the dingo comes back, this time closer than ever! The monitor tries another lunge. The dingo doesn't run away. He sniffs a little closer.

The monitor does the next best thing. He runs. He scampers up a tree and presses himself flat on a branch. The dingo eyes him from below and then leaves—finally. That was close.

The Gould's monitor may be frightened by large animals such as the dingo. But he's quite the predator himself. He has sharp teeth and claws. And as some snakes do, he can swallow his prey whole. *Last night for dinner, the monitor ate . . .*

... a young carpet python slithering across the sand. To see what another carpet python is up to, TURN TO PAGE 18.

... a marsupial mole found under a rock. To see what another marsupial mole is up to, TURN TO PAGE 36.

... a water-holding frog just waking up. To see what another water-holding frog is up to, TURN TO PAGE 52.

... a western barred bandicoot scratching in the dirt. To see what another western barred bandicoot is up to, TURN TO PAGE 56.

... a European wild rabbit digging a new burrow. To see what another European wild rabbit is up to, TURN TO PAGE 46.

... a red kangaroo, after it was hit by a car. To see what another red kangaroo is up to, TURN TO PAGE 40.

... a tawny frogmouth with a hurt wing. To see what another tawny frogmouth is up to, TURN TO PAGE 14.

... a dead short-beaked echidna. To see what another short-beaked echidna is up to, TURN TO PAGE 58.

WATER-HOLDING FROG *(Cyclorana platycephala)*

A burst of rain sprinkles down on the hard dry earth of the Outback. It hasn't rained here in almost six months. The water starts to collect and soak into the ground. Two feet (0.6 meters) down, it dampens a grayish green blob. The blob stirs. No, it's not a pocket of mud. It's a water-holding frog, and she's just coming out of a deep resting stage.

First, she starts to breath deeper and her heart beats faster. Then she starts munching her cocoon, or covering of skin. Before she went underground, she sucked up as much water as possible into her plump body. Then, deep underground, she built a cocoon around herself from her own skin. It helped her to keep the water inside her body. Who knew how long she'd be underground? In the Outback, it can go for years without raining. But since it's finally rained, the frog wakes again. The cocoon is her first meal in six months.

With her huge back legs, she digs her way back to the Outback surface. The rain has cleared, but there are still puddles around. And the **billabong** is filled again. With a snoringlike noise, she calls for a male water-holding frog. She needs a mate and has to work fast. In the heat of the Outback, those puddles will soon disappear.

After mating, she will lay her eggs in a pocket of water near the billabong. Her tadpoles will be in a race to survive—they'll need to develop into fully formed frogs by the time the water disappears.

Now, it's on to finding a real meal. *The water-holding frog chomps down . . .*

52

Frog Water

Australia's native people are known as the Aborigines. Aborigines have lived in the Outback for tens of thousands of years. They know many ways to survive in the Outback. Aborigines know that the water-holding frog can be used as a source of emergency water. They will find and dig up frogs. The frog has stored its water in its bladder. So an Aborigine will simply put the back of the frog in his mouth and squeeze the water out for a drink. Ah, refreshing.

... **crickets hopping through the grass.** To see what other crickets are up to, TURN TO PAGE 57.

... **bush flies buzzing around the water's edge.** To see what other bush flies are up to, TURN TO PAGE 45.

GHOST BAT *(Macroderma gigas)*

As dusk falls, the ghost bat emerges from a crevice in the rock. Behind her, a stream of other female bats follows. This is a girls-only colony. The boys have their own roost.

She flaps to a familiar tree. In the growing darkness, pale fur on her back and front give her a ghostly look. That's where the ghost bat gets its name. She finds her usual perch and promptly hangs upside down, folding her wings around her carefully.

She may look at rest, but really she's hunting. Her excellent hearing and vision are just the tools she'll need when the opportunity arises. And here it comes!

At the base of the tree, a mouse scurries around a tuft of grass. He thinks he's safe in the dark, but up above, the bat is alert. Silently, she drops down. The mouse never even sees her coming. His world suddenly goes dark as the ghost bat wraps her wings tightly around him. Then she finishes him off—by biting him in the neck. It's no wonder that ghost bats are sometimes called Australian giant false vampire bats!

The bat carries her dead prey up to the top of the tree to eat it. She's a sloppy eater. In fact, you can tell where ghost bats roost by the mess of bones below on the ground.

Last night for dinner, the ghost bat swooped down to attack . . .

. . . a frilled lizard crawling across a rock. To see what another frilled lizard is up to, TURN TO PAGE 12.

. . . a water-holding frog that just laid her eggs. To see what another water-holding frog is up to, TURN TO PAGE 52.

. . . lots of bush flies. To see what other bush flies are up to, TURN TO PAGE 45.

. . . a baby Gould's monitor hunting for the first time. To see what another Gould's monitor is up to, TURN TO PAGE 49.

. . . a couple of crickets. To see what other crickets are up to, TURN TO PAGE 57.

WESTERN BARRED BANDICOOT
(Perameles bougainville)

The hidden grass nest under that bush is empty. It used to be the home of a western barred bandicoot, but the animal has been gone for a while. Foxes and cats, which are not native to the Outback, have found the western barred bandicoot a little too easy to catch. And now these tiny, furry **mammals** are almost impossible to find. That's why this is a *DEAD END*.

Western barred bandicoots are threatened by the increased clearing of the Outback. Clearing occurs when humans cut down trees and uproot plants. Humans clear land to make room for farms and buildings. But without plant life, bandicoots are in trouble. They make their nests under shrubs, and they eat berries, seeds, and plant roots. They also eat the earthworms and insects found near plants.

CRICKETS
(Orthoptera gryllidae)

Darkness falls and the day cools. The cricket rouses in his burrow under dead wattle leaves. First, his long antennae emerge. Then his four small front legs and four wings unfold. Once his giant back legs are out, he pushes off and springs through the air. He lands 3 feet (0.9 meters)away. That's quite a jump for something his size. Imagine if you could jump 80 feet (24 m) from a standstill!

57

Once out in the open, he starts his singing. But he doesn't sing with his mouth. The edge of his hind legs are lined with a row of little barbs. He drags the barbs against his front wings to make a rhythmic sound. Chirp. Chirp. Chirp. He calls for a female.

Scientists have studied the chirps of crickets. They learned that the warmer the weather, the faster crickets chirp. Scientists have figured mathematical formulas that use cricket sounds to tell the temperature.

If a female is out there listening, she'll hear his call through her knees. That's where cricket ears are—in the knees of their front legs.

But no one answers tonight. So he's off to do his next job of the evening— eat some food. *Last night for dinner, the cricket nibbled on...*

...dead leaves and grass.
To see what the plants of the Outback are like, TURN TO PAGE 24.

SHORT-BEAKED ECHIDNA *(Tachyglossus aculeatus)*

The short-beaked echidna shuffles along the ground. Her spiny body sways with each step. At a large stone, she pauses. She shoves her beak under the edge of the stone and flips it. Her beak is covered in skin. She needs that beak to get at food. If it gets damaged, she'll die.

The echidna has a 7-inch-long (18-centimeter) wormlike tongue. Imagine having a tongue half as long as your body! With her tongue, she slurps up the insects hiding under the stone. She crushes the insects against the spikes in the top of her mouth. Then she can swallow them. She doesn't have teeth to chew the bugs nor any stomach juices to dissolve them. When the food gets to her stomach, a hairy rough lining grinds up the food for digestion.

An echidna uses its tongue to grab termites.

But she's not done eating. With her strong front claws, she rakes at the ground. Soon dirt is flying. She sticks her beak in—and gets a noseful of dirt. No matter. She clears it with a couple of puffs of air (and a snot bubble) and keeps after those hidden bugs. You can hear her from yards away. And a Gould's monitor has just turned her way. . . .

Even though the echidna has no outer ears, she has excellent hearing. She hears the monitor approach. She tucks her head in and rolls up. He nudges her, but there's nothing he can do with that ball of spikes. He soon lumbers away.

She stretches out again. Her spikes, or spines, are not like those of a porcupine or a hedgehog. Each of her spines is attached to muscles. She can move them like fingers. She uses them to climb or to roll herself over. Imagine being able to move each hair on your head whenever you want!

Right now she uses her spines to get herself into a sitting position. She lays a marble-sized egg and then rolls it up her soft tummy to tuck it into her pouch. The echidna is a **marsupial**, meaning that her baby will finish growing inside a pouch on her body.

The echidna is also a **mammal**—an animal that feeds her young with milk from her body. But she is a very unusual mammal. Most mammals give birth to a live baby. But the echidna lays eggs. Egg-laying mammals are called **monotremes**. The echidna is one of only two monotremes in the world. (The other is a platypus, an Australian water animal.) Her baby will hatch from the egg and remain in her pouch until it grows spines and can survive on its own.

In the meantime, she's got to feed herself. *Last night for dinner, she dug up more worms and bugs such as . . .*

Echidna Spines

Echidna spines are very strong. They've been known to puncture car tires when the cars have accidentally hit echidnas. The spines protect the echidnas from nearly all predators. But some dingoes have figured out a way around those spines. When the echidna balls up, the dingo will urinate on its face. This makes the echidna unroll, and the dingo attacks its soft belly.

. . . crickets. To see what other crickets are up to, TURN TO PAGE 67.

GLOSSARY

bacteria: tiny living things made up of only one cell

billabong: in the Outback, a pool of water similar to a large pond

carnivore: an animal that eats other animals

carrion: the bodies of animals that have died or were killed by predators that are eaten by other animals as food

cold-blooded: a term for animals that use outside energy, such as heat from the sun, to warm their body temperature

decompose: to decay, or break down, after dying

decomposers: living things, such as insects or bacteria, that feed on dead plants and animals

endangered: at risk of becoming extinct

extinct: no longer existing

food chain: a system in which energy is transferred from the sun to plants and to animals as each eats and is eaten

food web: many food chains linked together

habitats: areas where a plant or animal naturally lives and grows

hatchlings: young animals newly hatched from eggs

herbivores: animals that eat plants

maggots: the larvas of certain insects, such as flies

mammals: animals that have hair and feed their babies milk from their bodies

marsupial: a mammal that gives birth to a live baby very early in the baby's development. A marsupial baby finishes growing in a pouch on the outside of its mother's body.

minerals: substances found in nature that animals need to survive

monotremes: egg-laying mammals

nutrients: substances, especially in food, that help a plant or animal survive

predators: animals that hunt and kill other animals for food

primary consumers: animals that eat plants

producers: living things that make their own food

reptiles: cold-blooded, egg-laying animals with backbones

secondary consumers: animals and insects that eat other animals and insects

tertiary consumers: animals that eat other animals and that have few natural enemies

FURTHER READING AND WEBSITES

Australian (and Nearby Islands) Animal Printouts
http://www.enchantedlearning.com/coloring/Australia.shtml
Enchanted Learning's website is full of simple information, puzzles, quizzes, and coloring sheets of your favorite Outback animals.

Australia's Endangered Animals
http://www.kidcyber.com.au/topics/Austendangered.htm
Learn about some of Australia's endangered animals and what is threatening them.

Burt, Denise. *Kangaroos*. Minneapolis: Lerner Publications Company, 2000. As part of the Nature Watch series, Burt's book looks at the Outback's most famous marsupial.

Lewin, Ted, and Betsy Lewin. *Top to Bottom*. New York: HarperCollins, 2005. This husband and wife children's author-illustrator team chronicle their travels through Australia with cartoons as well as realistic watercolor illustrations.

Markle, Sandra. *Tasmanian Devils*. Minneapolis: Lerner Publications Company, 2005. This book in the Animal Scavenger series looks at the life cycle and habits of Tasmania's unique marsupials.

Parish, Steve. *Australia Rare and Endangered Wildlife*. Broomall, PA: Mason Crest Publishers, 2003. This book features one-page profiles on many of the animals of Australia that are fighting to survive.

Perth Zoo: Australian Bushwalk
http://www.perthzoo.wa.gov.au/Animals--Plants/Australia/Australian-Bushwalk/
Australia's Perth Zoo features the Australian Bushwalk—a tour of the country's many habitats. Visitors to the zoo website can take a virtual bushwalk and find photographs and profiles of many Outback animals.

Wild Kids: Arid Zone
http://www.amonline.net.au/wild_kids/arid_zone.cfm
The Australia Museum's website looks at the different physical features of the Outback and the animals who dwell there.

SELECTED BIBLIOGRAPHY

AustralianFauna.com. 2006. http://www.australianfauna.com/ (July 3, 2008).

Australian Government. "Threatened Species and Ecological Communities." *Department of the Environment, Water, Heritage, and the Arts. Resources.* 2008. http://www.environment.gov.au/biodiversity/threatened/ (August 8, 2008).

Australian Wildlife Conservancy. N.d. http://www.australianwildlife.org/ (July 3, 2008).

Burnie, David. *Animal: The Definitive Visual Guide to the World's Wildlife.* New York: DK, 2005.

Franklin, Adrian. *Animal Nation: The True Story of Animals and Australia.* Sydney: University of New South Wales Press, 2006.

Mattison, Chris. *Lizards of the World.* New York: Facts on File, 2004.

————. *Frogs and Toads of the World.* New York: Facts on File, 1992.

New South Wales Government, Department of Environment and Climate Change. "Native Plants and Animals." *National Parks and Wildlife Service.* 2008. http://www.nationalparks.nsw.gov.au/npws.nsf/Content/Native+plants+and+animals (July 2, 2008).

Smith, Roff. *Australia: Journey through a Timeless Land.* Washington, DC: National Geographic Books, 1999.

Tasmania. "Native Plants and Animals." *Department of Primary Industries and Water.* 2008. http://www.dpiw.tas.gov.au/inter.nsf/ThemeNodes/SSKA-4X33SG (July 3, 2008).

INDEX

Photo Acknowledgments

The images in this book are used with the permission of: © Doug Armand/Stone/Getty Images, pp. 1, 11, 13, 15, 19, 23, 26, 33, 39, 51, 53, 55; © John W Banagan/Iconica/Getty Images, pp. 4–5, 6–7; © Roland Seitre/Peter Arnold, Inc., p. 8; © Martin Harvey/NHPA/Photoshot, pp. 9, 48; © Jean-Paul Ferrero/AUSCAPE, pp. 10, 16, 42; © Belinda Wright/National Geographic/Getty Images, pp. 12, 22; © A.N.T. Photo Library/NHPA/Photoshot, pp. 14 (top), 20, 25 (bottom), 35, 45, 49; © Gerry Ellis/Minden Pictures/Getty Images, pp. 14 (bottom), 24 (top); © Konrad Wothe/Minden Pictures/Getty Images, pp. 17, 41; © Jerry Dupree/Dreamstime.com, p. 18; © Daniel Zupanc/NHPA/Photoshot, p. 21; © Howard Rice/Gap Photo/Visuals Unlimited, p. 24 (bottom); © Thorsten Milse/Robert Harding World Imagery/Getty Images, p. 27 (top); © Ann & Steve Toon/NHPA/Photoshot , p. 27 (bottom); © ZSSD/Minden Pictures/Getty Images, p. 28; © Theo Allofs/Visuals Unlimited, p. 29; © Frank Woerle/AUSCAPE, p. 30; © Dave Watts/NHPA/Photoshot, pp. 31, 59; © Stephen Dalton/NHPA/Photoshot, p. 32 (top); © D. Parer & E. Parer-Cook/AUSCAPE, pp. 32 (bottom), 52; © Nicholas Birks/AUSCAPE, pp. 36, 38; © Jean-Jacques Alcalay-BIOSPHOTO/AUSCAPE, p. 37; © Mitsuaki Iwago/Minden Pictures/Getty Images, p. 40; © Ted Mead/The Image Bank/Getty Images, p. 43; © Jason Edwards/National Geographic/Getty Images, p. 44; © R. Usher/WILDLIFE/Peter Arnold, Inc., p. 46; © S. Muller/WILDLIFE/Peter Arnold, Inc., p. 47; © NHPA/Photoshot, pp. 50, 54; © Babs Wells/Oxford Scientific/Photolibrary, p. 56; © Roland Seitre/Peter Arnold, Inc., p. 57; © iStockphoto.com/Phil Morley, p. 58 (top); © Kathie Atkinson/AUSCAPE, p. 58 (bottom). Illustrations and map: © Bill Hauser/Independent Picture Service.

Front cover: © Doug Armand/Stone/Getty Images (landscape); © A.N.T. Photo Library/NHPA/Photoshot (crocodile); © Mitsuaki Iwago/Minden Pictures/Getty Images (kangaroos); © James Hager/Robert Harding World Imagery/Getty Images (emu); © iStockphoto.com/Jeremy Edwards (koala).

About the Authors

Don Wojahn and Becky Wojahn are school library media specialists by day and writers by night. Their natural habitat is the temperate forests of northwestern Wisconsin, where they share their den with two animal-loving sons and two big black dogs. The Wojahns' other Follow That Food Chain books include *A Temperate Forest Food Chain*, *A Desert Food Chain*, *A Rain Forest Food Chain*, *A Savanna Food Chain*, and *A Tundra Food Chain*.